GREAT INVENTIONS

THE PHONOGRAPH

By Robin Doak

WORLD ALMANAC® LIBRARY

Please visit our web site at: www.worldalmanaclibrary.com
For a free color catalog describing World Almanac® Library's list of high-quality books
and multimedia programs, call 1-800-848-2928 (USA) or 1-800-387-3178 (Canada).
World Almanac® Library's fax: (414) 332-3567.

Library of Congress Cataloging-in-Publication Data

Doak, Robin S. (Robin Santos), 1963-
    The phonograph / by Robin Doak.
       p. cm. — (Great inventions)
    Includes bibliographical references and index.
    ISBN 0-8368-5877-8 (lib. bdg.)
    ISBN 0-8368-6587-1 (softcover)
    1. Phonograph—Juvenile literature. I. Title. III. Great inventions
(Milwaukee, Wis.)
    TS2301.P3D57   2005
    621.389'33—dc22   2005041610

First published in 2006 by
World Almanac® Library
A Member of the WRC Media Family of Companies
330 West Olive Street, Suite 100
Milwaukee, WI 53212 USA

Copyright © 2006 by World Almanac® Library.

A Creative Media Applications, Inc. Production
Design and Production: Alan Barnett, Inc.
Editor: Susan Madoff
Copy editor: Laurie Lieb
Proofreaders: Tania Bissell, Laurie Lieb
Indexer: Nara Wood
World Almanac® Library editor: Carol Ryback
World Almanac® Library art direction: Tammy West
World Almanac® Library production: Jessica Morris

Photo credits: Clip Art: pages 4, 10, 15, 29; Associated Press Worldwide: pages 7, 13, 14, 24, 31,
35, 41, 42; © The Granger Collection: pages 8, 16; © Hulton-Deutsch Collection/CORBIS:
page 11; © Getty Images/Hulton Archive: pages 20, 23, 37; Photo.com: pages 26, 36;
© Mitchell Gerber/CORBIS: page 21, © Bettmann/CORBIS: page 22; diagrams by Rolin Graphics.

All rights reserved. No part of this book may be reproduced, stored in a retrieval system,
or transmitted in any form or by any means, electronic, mechanical, photocopying, recording,
or otherwise, without the prior written permission of the copyright holder.

Printed in the United States of America

1 2 3 4 5 6 7 8 9 09 08 07 06 05

TABLE OF CONTENTS

Words that appear in the glossary are printed in
boldface type the first time they appear in the text.

NOW HEAR THIS!

A world without stereos, CD players, and other sound recording and playing devices would be bleak indeed. Imagine holiday shopping without festive carols playing in the background, exercising without the driving beat of a "techno" song, or going to a baseball game without listening to a tape-recorded national anthem. Even movies would be silent.

The **phonograph**, tape recorder, and other sound recording devices have also helped bring the past to life. Historians and sound engineers have created an audible record of American life through the past decades. Recorded stories of immigrants, Native Americans, and important politicians and public figures have enhanced the understanding and appreciation of history. Listening to music and stories on disk and on tape gives people a better understanding of forgotten times and different cultures. Everyday sounds that are fading from memory, such as the clicking of typewriter keys, can also be preserved forever.

Sound recording devices have also improved the way humans communicate with each other. Answering machines ensure that people don't miss important messages.

▼ The phonautograph invented by Edouard-Leon Scott de Martinville, produced visual images of sound but could not play them aloud.

Saving the Sounds of the Past

In 1948, Moses Asch, the founder of Folkways Music, began recording the sounds of everyday life. When he wasn't recording folk songs, he recorded elevators, jackhammers, and mosquitoes, sounds that most people took for granted.

In 1986, Asch donated his collection to the Smithsonian Institute in Washington, D.C. The collection was added to other sound recordings in the museum to create a unique record of America's past and present. Today, the sounds of a nation are all housed in a bomb-proof vault. These sounds are also available for sale through the museum. For example, a CD called *Sounds of the Office* includes sounds that are rarely heard anymore: an adding machine, an old-time telephone ring, and an electric typewriter.

Books, letters, and miscellaneous information can be recorded on tape.

The invention of the phonograph and related recording devices created billion-dollar industries— and millions of jobs. People who benefit from this technology include musicians, singers, songwriters, sound engineers, journalists, computer technicians, and many others. Sound recording devices helped create pop stars. Today, Alicia Keys and Usher can thank the phonograph and its ever-evolving technology for their superstardom.

Before the Phonograph

About 1856, a French printer named Edouard-Leon Scott de Martinville (1817–1879) invented a device he called the **phonautograph.** Scott's machine recorded sound waves and produced a visual image of the sound. The device could not, however, play or reproduce any sounds.

Scott's phonautograph included a device made of brass that funneled sound waves from the larger end toward a small, thin membrane stretched across the

A Mechanical Ear

When creating his phonautograph, Scott used the human ear as his model. The brass horn of his device served the same purpose as the auricle (fleshy ear flap) of the outer ear. The membrane performed the same job as the eardrum (tympanic membrane).

narrow end. The sound waves caused the flexible membrane to vibrate, which in turn caused a short, stiff hog hair on the other side of the membrane to also vibrate and move. The hog hair acted as a **stylus,** or pen, graphing a wavy line on a piece of smoke-blackened glass. Later, the glass was replaced with smoked paper attached to a revolving cylinder.

Scott had no success marketing his instrument. Although the phonautograph was an interesting device, few people—other than scientists—had any real need or desire to create sound graphs. Although Scott's invention did not re-create sound, his work inspired other inventors to find a way to replay these captured sound waves.

The Phonograph Is Almost Invented

In April 1877, a French inventor named Charles Cros (1842–1888) wrote a paper describing a machine for recording and replaying sound. Cros's invention worked on the same principle as Scott's device, but took the phonautograph to the next level. Cros suggested that the squiggly line drawn on the blackened paper be etched onto a material such as steel. In order to reproduce sound from the steel, Cros proposed running a metallic point, or needle, over it, thus sending the sound back through the membrane and out through the horn so that anyone in the room could hear it.

Cros, who was also a part-time poet and scientist, had hit upon the first effective design for a phonograph. Unfortunately, no one in France was willing to invest the money Cros needed to obtain a patent for his design. (A patent is a license from a government that gives a person the sole rights to make and sell an invention for a certain amount of time.) Cros could do little but talk about his machine and show his plans to those who were interested. One admirer, Abbé Lenoir, called Cros's device a phonograph, from the Greek words that mean "sound writer." Cros, however, called his invention the paleograph.

Cros tried to protect his plan by submitting it to L'Académie de Sciences in Paris. Less than a year later, however, he would watch with disappointment as U.S. inventor Thomas Alva Edison (1847–1931) built the first working phonograph. Both phonographs operated on the same principles. Unlike Edison's plans, Cros's plans called for transferring sound waves to a disk of blackened glass.

▼ *Thomas Alva Edison envisioned many uses for the phonograph, including dictation, recording books, and eventually playing music.*

Mary Had a Little Lamb

Although Cros was the first person to come up with the idea of the phonograph, Edison was the first to build a device that recorded and reproduced sound. Edison's device, built in late 1877, was similar in design to the phonautograph. The New Jersey inventor called his new machine the phonograph. It is not known whether Edison borrowed the name from Lenoir or came up with it independently. Instead of using smoke-blackened glass or paper, the first phonograph used a revolving cylinder covered with heavy tinfoil.

To work the machine, one person cranked a handle that turned the foil-covered cylinder while a second person shouted into the horn. The phonograph's stylus, or needle, then recorded the sound waves as indentations on the tinfoil. A second stylus attached to the membrane (also called a diaphragm) played back the sounds. As the needle moved over the tinfoil "record," it made the membrane vibrate. The vibrating membrane produced sounds similar to those that had been recorded.

The first words that Edison recorded on his phonograph were "Mary had a little lamb." The quality of this and other early recordings was very poor. Sheets of tinfoil did not create high-quality recordings and weren't durable enough to withstand being played more than a few times. In addition, only people who had been specially trained to operate the machines could play these earliest phonographs. Inventors began looking for a material that was more suitable for recording. They hoped to build a better phonograph.

Despite the first phonograph's flaws, Edison saw many potential uses for the new machine. He believed that businesses could use the phonograph for taking notes and dictating letters and that blind people could use it to hear books. He also looked forward to a time when musicians would use his invention to record music. In early 1878, Edison established the Edison Speaking Phonograph Company to manufacture and sell the phonograph. Edison then turned his attention to other inventions.

▲ A poster from the late 1800s features an advertisement for one of the products sold by the Edison Speaking Phonograph Company.

The Phonograph

From Tinfoil to Wax

Other inventors quickly picked up where Edison left off. One such person was Alexander Graham Bell (1847–1922), a Scottish-born inventor who had recently created a device known as the telephone. In 1880, Bell founded a company in Washington, D.C., with two others: Bell's cousin, Chichester Bell (1848–1924), a chemical engineer, and Charles Tainter (1854–1940).

In the early and mid-1880s, Chichester Bell and Tainter found a number of ways to improve Edison's invention. One of the most important innovations was to replace tinfoil cylinders with cardboard ones coated with wax. The two also pioneered a "floating" stylus, a needle that moved freely with sound waves to create cuts instead of dents in the wax. They received a patent for the improved device, which they called a **graphophone**, in May 1886.

Edison worried that Bell and Tainter would take credit for his invention. Once again, he turned his attention back to the phonograph. In 1888, Edison created two improved versions of his first phono-graph, which he named the Improved Phonograph and the Perfected Phonograph. Like the graphophone, Edison's new machines used wax-coated cylinders. Although wax was an improvement over tinfoil, the

The Wizard of Menlo Park

Thomas Alva Edison was one of the greatest inventors of all time. In addition to the phonograph, Edison also invented electric lighting and made important improvements to the telegraph, telephone, and motion pictures. He received nearly 1,100 patents from the U.S. Patent Office—more than any other single person. His inventions revolutionized communication and improved the quality of life in the United States and around the world.

new cylinders could still not be mass-produced. (Mass production is the making of goods in large quantities.)

One man who saw the potential of the new inventions was businessman Jesse Lippincott. Lippincott took control of the phonograph market by buying up the companies that made the machines and combining them to form the North American Phonograph Company. He also purchased the rights to sell both graphophones and phonographs. One company that Lippincott bought was the American Graphophone Company, the first company formed to sell Bell and Tainter's graphophone. The company's factory in Bridgeport, Connecticut, produced as many as four graphophones a day.

Lippincott focused on the business uses of the phonograph, marketing it as a dictation machine rather than a device for listening to music. In the late 1800s, the United States was suffering from economic hardship, and few businesses bought the new, untested devices. Sales of the phonograph—an invention that seemed so promising—were disappointing.

▼ *The cardboard and wax cylinders on Chichester Bell and Charles Tainter's graphophone played for about ten minutes, as opposed to the two to three minutes, playing time of the tinfoil cylinders on Thomas Edison's phonograph.*

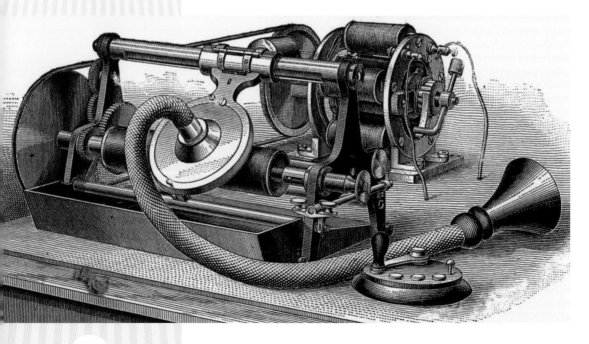

MUSIC FOR THE MASSES

In the 1890s, Edison and his rivals, Bell and Tainter, became interested in the possible entertainment value of the phonograph. Several of the earliest patents that the inventors submitted were for coin-operated phonograph machines that could play recorded music at saloons, in arcades, and even on ferryboats. These earliest jukeboxes provided instant entertainment and were wildly successful.

By the late 1890s, the price of a phonograph dropped low enough to make the machines affordable for many Americans. In 1899, spring-driven motors made it possible for people to purchase an Edison phonograph for $7.50 (about $165 in today's money). At this time, a phonograph factory existed in almost every major U.S. city. The goal of Edison's and other phonograph companies was evident: Advertising for Edison's phonograph company showed a picture of the inventor with the slogan, "I want a phonograph in every home."

The First True Record

In 1887, a German immigrant named Emile Berliner (1851–1929) made improvements to the phonograph that revolutionized the machine. Combining the best elements

▼ *American inventor Emile Berliner pioneered the gramophone, the first phonograph to use flat disks as opposed to cylinders. Disks were more easily and inexpensively duplicated for mass production. He is pictured here with another of his inventions, the microphone, which was used in the first Bell telephones.*

Emile Berliner

In 1870, eighteen-year-old Emile Berliner emigrated from Germany to the United States. While working at a chemical research laboratory, Berliner became interested in science and inventing.

In Washington, D.C., Berliner set up a laboratory in his house. Here, he improved upon Alexander Graham Bell's telephone transmitter. Berliner's new transmitter, called a microphone, could increase the volume and improve the quality of a person's voice on the telephone.

In later years, Berliner continued his career as an inventor. In the early 1920s, he and his son, Henry, built one of the first successful helicopters. (Henry later founded the Berliner Aircraft Company.) Berliner was also involved in a number of social causes. In 1911, he established the Sarah Berliner Fellowship to give women the chance to perform scientific research. The scholarship is still awarded today.

of both Edison's and Chichester Bell's machines, Berliner pioneered a phonograph that recorded and played flat, disk-shaped records. His records—the first ever—were made of zinc. He also introduced a replaceable metal stylus to "read" the grooves in his records. Berliner had created the first record player, or turntable. A turntable is the round, revolving platform on a phonograph that records are placed on.

Perhaps the most important characteristic of the new flat disks was the ease of producing numerous copies of disks from the original master disk. Berliner created a master disk out of zinc. He covered the zinc disk with a thin, waxy film. Then he used a stylus to etch sound waves onto the film, then dipped the entire disk into an acid mixture. The acid ate through the zinc where the stylus had cut through the wax. Berliner used the resulting "master record" to create copies, or "records," of the music.

In late 1894, Berliner began selling his **gramophone,** as well as records to play on it, in Washington, D.C. Early records were 7 inches (18 centimeters) in diameter, with recordings on only one side. At first, they were made out of hard rubber or celluloid, a hard, transparent substance made from plants. Later, the records were made out of shellac, or varnish, and cotton fibers. The gramophone and its flat records were very popular and gave a big boost to the fledgling recording industry. Early popular gramophone music included marches and patriotic songs by the famous American composer and bandleader John Philip Sousa as well as selections from Will F. Denny, a comic singer. His songs, including "How Would You Like to Be the Ice Man" and "I'm Not Particular," were advertised by Berliner as "always funny and sure to amuse." The mid-1890s saw other important innovations that made the phonograph popular with people across the

◀ *Thomas Alva Edison exhibited the tinfoil phonograph at the National Academy of Science in Washington, D.C., and later demonstrated it for President Rutherford Hayes at the White House on April 18, 1878.*

country. For example, the hand crank and electric motors that powered older machines were replaced with a spring motor. A spring motor is a type of motor that can be wound up—like an old-fashioned clock.

The Birth of the Recording Industry

Because the phonograph could be used to both record and play music, amateur musicians with different degrees of talent soon began recording their own music and selling records. Music companies soon jumped on

Edison Accepts the Disk

In the early 1900s, Edison's associates realized that disks outperformed cylinders in every way. Afraid of offending their boss, the men began working on a disk phonograph in secret. When Edison discovered what his associates were up to, he embraced the task and began working on it himself. In 1912, the Edison Company began selling disk phonographs alongside the models that played cylinders. Edison's disk-shaped records could not be played on the phonographs made by the other two companies. By 1925, Edison's cylinder recordings were no longer available in stores. Customers had to order the cylinders directly from the Edison factory.

▲ *Bandleader John*
Philip Sousa (center,
with a black beard) and
the Marine Marching
Band (pictured here in
1890) were early stars
of the new recording
industry.

the bandwagon, mass-producing a variety of record-ings. Early records featured marches, opera pieces, and speeches. The recording industry had been born!

Before long, three companies stood out as the top producers of phonographs and recordings. The Edison Phonograph Company, founded by Edison and others, manufactured and sold phonographs that played recordings on cylinders. The Victor Talking Machine Company, founded by Eldridge Johnson, sold phono-graphs that played disk-shaped records. And the Columbia Phonograph Company sold both. In 1912, Columbia stopped producing recordings on cylinders and focused on producing disk-shaped records.

The Big Three, as the companies came to be known, quickly dominated the recording industry. Business was booming. The Big Three could barely keep up with the public's demand for phonographs and record-ings. Each company provided a line of phonographs, from small ones that sold for $10 to huge, furniture-like pieces that cost as much as $500. As phonograph sales increased, the demand for recordings to play on them increased as well. From 1897 to 1899, the sale of records jumped from 500,000 to 2.8 million.

The Big Three increased their sales by advertising their wares. The Victor Company ran one of the most successful ad campaigns. The ads showed a small fox

The Columbia Phonograph Company

The Columbia Phonograph Company got its start in 1889. The company sold graphophones as well as Edison's phonographs in Washington, D.C., Pennsylvania, and Maryland. Within a few years, Columbia began building its own phonographs—and recording its own records. In 1891, it published a catalog of phonographs and recordings available for purchase.

Columbia survived through the years by changing with the industry. In 1901, for example, the company began selling phonographs that played the disk records pioneered by Emile Berliner. Customers paid fifty cents for 7-inch (18-cm) records and one dollar for 10-inch (25-cm) records. In 1908, Columbia introduced double-sided records to Americans.

Today, Columbia is known as Columbia Records, a part of Sony BMG. Columbia is the oldest continuously used brand-name in the recording industry. Artists who record under the Columbia Records label include Aerosmith, Beyonce, and John Mayer.

terrier listening to a phonograph recording. The motto beneath the picture read, "His Master's Voice."

In the early 1920s, manufacturers began placing paper labels in the center of the disk. Because early recordings were of such poor quality, early labels carried song lyrics so that people would know what they were listening to. Other early one-sided disks were stamped *L* for "left" and *R* for "right" so buyers knew which side to play. Unique and distinctive labels, or "seals," became a quick way to recognize a particular company or series of recordings. The Victor Company sold a line of records—stamped with a red label—recorded by favorite opera singers of the Russian czar. The line became known as Red-Seal records. Edison's company produced disks with his picture on the label.

▼ When the English artist Francis Barraud painted his dog, Nipper, listening to an antique phonograph, he had no idea that his whimsical painting would become one of the most recognizable trademarks in history. Purchased by the Victor Talking Machine Company in 1901, the image would eventually belong to RCA when they bought the company and trademark in 1929.

Victor
"HIS MASTER'S VOICE"
REG. U.S. PAT. OFF.
To insure Victor quality always look for the famous trademark "His Master's Voice" It is on all products of the Victor Talking Machine Company.

▼ *The kinetoscope record of* Fred Ott's Sneeze *illustrates the individual frames that made up Thomas Edison's first short film, shown to the public in 1893. The frames follow a vertical path depicting the actions of a man sneezing.*

In 1888, Thomas Alva Edison wrote a letter to the U.S. Patent Office, claiming that he was "experimenting upon an instrument that does for the eye what the phonograph does for the ear, which is the recording and reproduction of things in motion." Three years later, the inventor introduced the Kinetoscope, the first motion picture viewer.

On May 9, 1893 Edison showed off his new invention at the Brooklyn Institute in Brooklyn, New York. Viewers peered through a peephole in the big, bulky device to watch a ninety-second black-and-white film called *Fred Ott's Sneeze*. The short film included no sound but featured the first movie close-up. It was also the first movie to be copyrighted.

Americans were fascinated with Edison's new creation, and kinetoscope parlors popped up from coast to coast. The privilege of viewing one of Edison's films cost a nickel. People visiting the parlors could also use their coins to listen to the latest tunes on a phonograph.

Over the years, the Edison Manufacturing Company produced more than three hundred movies for the kinetoscope. At first, the movies showed famous people and scenic attractions. Movies of important news events kept viewers up-to-date on current events. For example, the Kinetoscope gave Americans their first views of President McKinley's inauguration, the Spanish-American War, and the San Francisco fire of 1906. Later, the company began making dramas and comedies. One of the most famous early films created by Edison and company was *The Great Train Robbery*, released in 1903.

Although the Kinetoscope was popular, it was quickly replaced by the film projection machine, called the **cinematograph** by its French inventors. These new machines projected the film's image onto a screen, allowing many people to view the moving pictures at the same time. These early movies were still silent. Sometimes, movie theaters hired live actors to read the dialogue that went along with a movie. Later, subtitles were added. Also, a piano player or orchestra might have provided background music.

In 1894, Edison tried to add sound to his Kinetoscope. The new invention, called a Kinetophone, was actually a Kinetoscope with a phonograph inside. People listened to the sound through rubber ear tubes connected to the phonograph. The Kinetoscope and phonograph were connected by a belt in an effort to make the film and sound run together. One of the earliest movies made by Edison using the Kinetophone showed a man playing a violin while two men danced along to the music.

In 1913, Edison introduced an improved version of his Kinetophone. The new device added sound to movies as the images were projected onto a screen.

W.K.L. Dickson

Although Edison is credited with inventing the Kinetoscope, his assistant, William Kennedy Laurie Dickson (1860–1935), actually built and perfected the device. As a teenager, Dickson traveled from England to work with Edison as a lab photographer. He began experimenting with celluloid film to create a series of images.

In 1893, Dickson built the Kinetographic Theater, Edison's film studio. The studio, built for $600, was nicknamed the Black Maria because it looked like the police wagons used to take people to jail. These vehicles were known as "Black Marias." The theater was mounted on a movable device that allowed the entire building to be turned to catch the sunlight throughout the day. Two years later, however, Dickson left Edison's company to strike out on his own. In 1896, Dickson told the world what he thought of his amazing invention. He wrote, "It is the crown and flower of nineteenth-century magic."

A Day with Thomas A. Edison

One of the many films made by Thomas Edison was *A Day with Thomas A. Edison,* released in 1922. The silent film, complete with subtitles, begins with Edison being chauffeured to his Invention Factory in West Orange, New Jersey. The first caption tells viewers that "Mr. Edison does not think his many notable inventions are enough; and at seventy-four years of age he is as actively as ever seeking better ways to do things."

The Kinetophone was attached to the projector with a pulley. That same year, Edison and his company filmed nineteen Kinetophone movies. Unfortunately, the Kinetophone was still far from perfect: Audiences often saw movies and **sound tracks** that weren't matched with each other. People began to complain about the quality of Edison's films. By 1918, the Edison Company had turned away from the talking-picture business.

Stars of the Silent Screen

In the early 1900s, movies became a popular form of entertainment for people across the country. Americans could visit arcades, saloons, and music halls to view the moving pictures. Soon, theaters dedicated to showing movies were built. Because most charged five cents for admission, such a theater became known as a nickelodeon. By 1908, there were as many as ten thousand nickelodeons across the country. Fairs and carnivals also carried movie projectors with them as they traveled from place to place, offering movies to customers in addition to the live shows.

People soon began demanding longer and more interesting movies, and an industry arose to meet the growing need. The new industry was centered on the West Coast, in a district of Los Angeles, California,

Fast Fact

Edison chose the name *kinetoscope* from the Greek words *kineto,* meaning "movement," and *scopos,* meaning "to watch." (The camera that made the motion pictures was called the **Kinetograph.**)

The Phonograph

known as Hollywood. Here, the warm, sunny weather made it possible to film year-round. The region also had a wide variety of natural scenery.

After World War I, movie actors gained popularity as their movies were shown throughout the United States and around the world. American women swooned over Italian immigrant Rudolph Valentino, while Theda Bara became Hollywood's first glamour girl. The best actors not only became silent screen stars and cultural icons, but also became quite wealthy. Some of the most popular silent actors included comedian Charlie Chaplin, Douglas Fairbanks, and Mary Pickford, "America's Sweetheart." (The three later founded a movie company called United Artists.)

The Talkies Take Over

In 1921, the first "talkie," or talking movie, was filmed. Called *Dream Street,* the movie included sound at the film's beginning. The sound was created by a system known as photokinema. Although the results were not entirely successful and the movie was not released to the public, talkies would soon transform the movie industry.

In 1923, inventor Lee de Forest introduced a film with a strip of sound recording on its edge. De Forest called this new type of sound-on-film technology **Phonofilm**. Although de Forest showed the short films he made in many theaters, he couldn't get any of the big movie studios interested in his invention.

In 1926, people across the United States got their first glimpse of talking movies. The Warner Brothers movie, *Don Juan,* included background music but not dialogue. A recorded disk synchronized to the movie produced music. Projectionists in movie

Fast Fact

One of the first motion pictures shown with a cinematograph was called *The Arrival of a Train.* The director shot the film so that it appeared as if the train came directly at the audience. As viewers watched the train approach them on-screen, many ran away in fright, fearing the image was a real train that could hit them.

▲ The popularity of talkies led to improvements in sound on film and an explosion of interest in the fledgling film industry.

theaters started the sound at a special spot at the beginning of the film. The new system, developed three years earlier, was known as **Vitaphone**.

The year 1927 was an important one for sound in movies. Warner Brothers released *The Jazz Singer* with Vitaphone. The feature-length film, starring Al Jolson, was a "part-talkie." It contained about twenty minutes of music as well as bits of dialogue spoken by the actor himself. Jack Warner, head of the studio, later recalled the viewers' reaction the first time Jolson spoke: They jumped to their feet cheering "as though they had been prodded with an electric stick."

The same year *The Jazz Singer* was released, the Fox Film Corporation developed an improved system of sound called **Movietone**. Movietone was an improved version of de Forest's Phonofilm. In this new system, the sound was included right on the film itself, next to the images. To showcase its new system, Fox Film released news films with sound. These newsreels, as they came to be known, quickly became an important way for people to learn what was going on around the world. In 1928, the first all-talking feature film, *City Lights*, made with a Movietone sound system, hit movie theaters across the country.

Once the public got a taste of talkies, the days of the silent film were over. In 1928, Paramount announced that it would stop making silent movies. By 1929, more people than ever before were visiting theaters to see the talking movies.

The Phonograph

For some silent stars, the birth of the talkies marked the death of their film careers. While some stars, including Greta Garbo, a glamorous movie idol from Sweden, were able to make the transition to talking movies, others found that the quality of their voices was unsuitable for films with sound. A new breed of actors—especially those who could sing— would quickly become the movie stars of the future.

Movies and Sound

The movie industry played an important role in advancing the state of sound recordings. In the 1920s, for example, movie sound engineers improved the quality of movie theater loudspeakers. In 1931, they introduced the three-way speaker system that eventually became the standard for all home stereo speakers. The three-way system separated sound into high, middle, and low frequencies. Different devices accurately transmitted the various sound waves. A woofer transmitted the lowest-frequency sounds, while a tweeter reproduced sounds with the highest frequency. A midrange driver transmitted sounds in the middle frequencies.

The public craze for talking movies, especially musicals, also helped the recording industry. People wanted to own records with the songs they had heard at movie theaters. Before long, recording companies were churning out hit records that featured the songs from movie musicals—a practice that continues today. Movie companies even began buying up recording companies.

▼ *The invention of the boom microphone improved the synchro- nization of sound and action on film. The position of the micro- phone, above the scene being photographed, but out of the frame, allows the actors freedom to move about naturally without compromising sound quality.*

▼ *Danish engineer Valdemar Poulsen paved the way for magnetic tape recording with his Telegraphone, invented in 1898, which made magnetic wire recordings.*

In 1898, Valdemar Poulsen (1869–1942), a Danish engineer, applied to the U.S. Patent Office to receive the sole rights to an unusual device he had invented for saving telephone messages. Poulsen's **Telegraphone** used an electromagnet to create a magnetic sound recording on steel wire. Poulsen had invented the earliest model for the tape recorder and answering machine.

Unfortunately, patent officials couldn't believe that Poulsen's invention could possibly work. They felt that the description of his device contradicted the understood principles of magnetism. The officials refused to give Poulsen a patent unless he traveled from Denmark to Washington, D.C., and demonstrated how his machine worked.

Eventually, U.S. patent officials allowed Poulsen to prove that his Telegraphone worked by testing it in front of witnesses in Europe. The inventor was finally awarded his patent in 1900 and began to manufacture the device.

In 1900, it looked as if the telegraphone would be a success. That year, Austrian emperor Franz Joseph recorded his voice on tape at the Paris Exposition (a kind of World's Fair). The quality of the recording was poor, however, and with the popularity of the phonograph growing rapidly, few Americans paid any attention to Poulsen's new device.

Tape Takes Off

In 1928, German engineer Fritz Pfleumer discovered a way to make lightweight paper tape coated with magnetic particles for sound recording. The new tape, sold with a recording machine called a **Magnetophon**, was excellent for taking dictation. But it was still not suited for recording music. The quality of a tape recording was still not as good as that of a phonograph.

During World War II, German companies improved and began mass-producing Magnetophons. The machines, now using plastic magnetic tape, allowed German dictator Adolf Hitler to record and spread Nazi propaganda throughout Germany and other countries that his army conquered. After U.S. troops captured a Magnetophon in 1944, American companies copied and began producing similar machines.

Entertainer Bing Crosby, who performed live weekly radio shows, was among the first performers to embrace the tape recorder. In 1947, he began tape-recording his radio shows and broadcasting them later. Crosby popularized this method among other radio performers, freeing them from the restrictions of producing live shows. By the 1950s, the radio industry was widely using tape recorders. Before long, recording companies such as Capitol Records also began using the new devices.

These early tape recorders were large machines with two separate reels. Magnetic tape that unwound from one reel was fed onto a second reel. As the tape

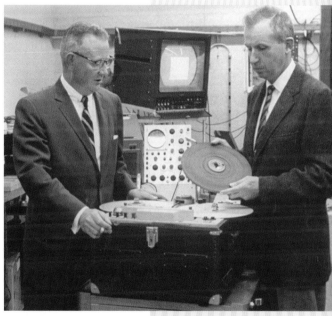

▲ The Magnetophon, shown here with two engineers, was used primarily for taking dictation. Its paper tape was later replaced with plastic tape that improved the quality of recording.

▲ A tape recorder used by President Richard M. Nixon while he was in office. The National Archives keeps taped records of White House business in order to preserve information that may be critical to the nation's interests and security.

traveled from reel to reel, small electromagnets, called "heads," recorded, erased, or played the sound signals.

Although the sound quality from a taped performance wasn't as good as one recorded on records, tape recorders were cheaper and easier to use. Tape recordings could also be edited by **splicing**—cutting out an unwanted part of the tape and rejoining the separated ends.

In 1958, eight-track tapes and players were introduced for the first time. Unlike reel-to-reel tapes, eight-track tapes ran in a continuous loop inside rectangular cartridges. "Eight-track" got its name from the four pairs of stereo (dual) **tracks** on the magnetic tape. A track is a strip that carries each separate recording.

Eight-track tape players and tapes were smaller and more portable than reel-to-reel tapes. The compact size of the players and tapes allowed people to take their favorite music with them in their cars. Car companies already knew that drivers enjoyed listening to the radio—surely drivers would also enjoy listening to selected artists on an eight-track player! Beginning in 1966, Ford became the first automobile company to offer the eight-track tape player as an option in its most expensive models.

The Answering Machine Catches On

Valdemar Poulsen developed the first working answering machine in the 1890s. In 1914, Edison made his contribution to the field with the invention of the Telescribe. This answering device captured telephone messages on a wax cylinder using Edison's phonograph dictating machine. Neither Poulsen's nor Edison's device became a commercial success.

In 1935, a smaller and more effective tape answering machine was built by Bell Laboratories. AT&T, the only telephone company in the United States at this time, did nothing to promote the machine, however. The company worried that using such a machine would violate the privacy of people making telephone calls. The company believed that worries over privacy might cause people to stop using the telephone.

Recording History: The American Folklife Center

Throughout the years, the phonograph and tape recorder have been used for more than just entertainment. Since the first wax cylinder recordings were made, historians have taken advantage of sound recording machines to protect America's rich heritage for future generations. Early recordings preserved the songs and folktales of Native American tribes and the oral histories of immigrants, factory workers, former slaves, politicians, military veterans, farmers—in short, Americans from every walk of life who built and shaped the nation over the years.

In 1928, the Library of Congress in Washington, D.C., began gathering recordings, photos, and written stories into a collection called the Archive of Folk Culture. Nearly fifty years later, the American Folklife Center was established by the U.S. Congress in order to oversee these important documents. Today, the center is home to more than four thousand collections from every part of the United States and around the world. For those who want to learn how average Americans lived or what they thought about, the American Folklife Center is a valuable research tool.

► A phonograph reveals the information recorded in the grooves on a record. A motor in the phonograph spins the turntable, which holds the vinyl disk, or record, in place on a rubber mat. The tone arm places the stylus along the grooves on the disk. As the stylus rides along the walls of the grooves, a transducer senses the motion and produces electric currents related to the movement. The transducer current is amplified and used to reproduce the recorded sound which is heard through speakers that are either part of the phonograph or attached by wires.

The rpm selector indicates at which speed (45, 78, or 33 1/3) the record you are playing needs to revolve. If the turntable is too slow, the pitch of the recording drops; if too fast, the pitch rises.

Phonograph

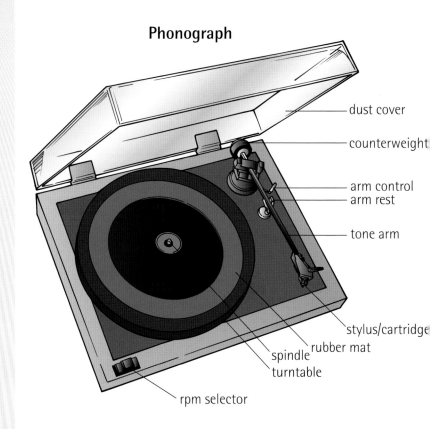

dust cover

counterweight

arm control
arm rest

tone arm

stylus/cartridge
rubber mat
spindle
turntable

rpm selector

Answering machines became popular office tools in the 1950s. Many doctors and other professionals began using the devices to record messages when they were out of the office. For many companies, buying or leasing these machines was cheaper than hiring an answering service or an assistant to take messages.

In the 1980s, purchases of home answering machines soared in the United States. The machines ensured that people no longer had to worry about missing important phone calls. The devices also gave people the ability to listen to whomever was calling before deciding whether or not to pick up the phone. Although answering machines are still popular, pagers, cellular phones, and caller ID makes it easier than ever to stay in touch with friends and relatives— and to avoid the calls of telemarketers.

5 THE RECORDING INDUSTRY

While the tape recorder was making inroads into the entertainment industry, the phonograph and disk records were also undergoing important changes. During the mid-1920s, for example, the Big Three introduced electrical recording. Instead of relying only on sound waves and styluses, companies began recording sounds with the help of microphones and electronic **amplifiers**. An amplifier is a device that increases the strength of an electrical signal.

Around this time, the Edison Company experimented with a 12-inch (30-cm) disk that played twenty minutes of music on each side. This was the first long-playing (LP) disk. Few people purchased Edison's LPs, however, and the company quickly stopped producing them.

Throughout the early 1900s, most records were made of a mixture of shellac and other materials, such as slate and limestone. They played at a speed of 78 revolutions per minute (**rpm**). In the 1940s, Columbia introduced a 16-inch (41-cm) vinyl record that played at a slower speed of 33⅓ rpm. The new LP could hold much more music on each side. And the new vinyl records were also sturdier than the

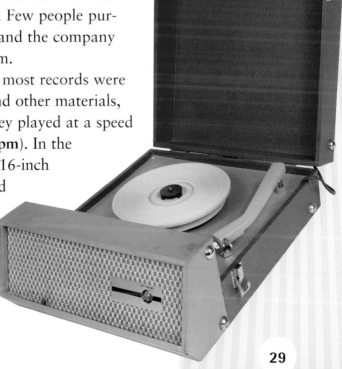

▼ Through the years, as record players became a staple of American homes and rock 'n' roll music became popular, portable turntables appealed to young people as a way to bring their music along when they gathered for entertainment.

V Disks

The 33⅓ rpm record was pioneered during World War II. The Office of War Information recorded popular music and messages from singers and bandleaders on these big disks for American troops fighting overseas. The records were called V disks: The *V* stood for victory. The records featured the music of Benny Goodman, Glenn Miller, Frank Sinatra, and many other artists. The V disks also included the sounds of everyday life, such as steaks being fried or traffic noise in New York City. Between 1943 and 1949, millions of V disks were sent to U.S. soldiers stationed around the world.

Fast Fact

The term *album* for a record originated during the early 1900s, when companies sold several records of long, classical pieces together in one paper-and-cardboard package. To hear the entire piece, listeners had to change disks.

shellac disks. The old 78s could be played only about 125 times before they were worn out by the needle scraping away tiny bits of shellac at each playing.

People who loved music loved the new LPs. The superior recordings captured by these records were so much closer to the original sounds that this system of recording came to be known as high-fidelity, or "hi-fi." Since that time, the phrase has continued to identify any recording equipment that has excellent recording capabilities.

In 1949, the Radio Corporation of America (RCA) introduced the 45-rpm record. RCA had taken over the Victor Company in 1929. The new disks quickly became popular with music lovers. By the late 1960s, few record companies produced the 78s, preferring the 45 and 33⅓ rpm formats.

In Stereo

In the early 1930s, recording companies tackled the challenge of making recordings sound more lifelike. While experimenting with different ideas, sound engineers laid the foundation for **stereophonic sound.** Stereophonic sound is recorded with two or more

The Phonograph

microphones, then played back on two or more speakers.

Sound engineers did not perfect stereophonic recording techniques until the late 1950s. At that time, companies began the mass production of stereo records. Within ten years, almost all records were recorded in stereophonic sound.

In the 1970s, engineers worked to further enhance sound recordings through **quadraphonic sound.** Quadraphonic sound is recorded with four different microphones and played back on four different speakers. Quadraphonic recordings made listeners feel as if they were surrounded with sound. Very few such recordings were made, however, and quadraphonic sound eventually faded away.

With advances in sound technology, home stereo systems became more popular. From the 1970s through the 1990s, home systems usually included a turntable, a tape player, a radio tuner and receiver, and speakers. The turntable itself consisted of a rotating platform, an arm, and a stylus. A special gear in the platform allowed listeners to change the rotation speed from 33⅓ rpm to 45 or 78 rpm. In this way, one record player could accommodate different types and sizes of records.

▲ A picture of the label attached to the acetate disk recorded as a demo by Elvis Presley for Sun Records in 1953.

The Birth of Rock 'n' Roll

The introduction of stereophonic sound and an improvement in the quality of sound recordings coincided with the birth of a new music genre: rock and roll, usually called *rock 'n' roll.* This new style combined elements of blues, country, and pop to create a distinct class of music, one that combined a strong, rhythmic beat and a simple melody. Electronic, stereophonic recordings made the booming rock beats and powerful electric-guitar chords sound great.

Rock 'n' roll struck a chord with young Americans, and the music soon became a sign of teenage rebellion. Later, rock artists in the late 1960s and early 1970s recorded songs of protest against the Vietnam War and other unpopular government policies. Modern musicians continue to use their art to express their feelings and frustrations about current events.

Like the music idols of today, some rock 'n' roll singers also became as popular as movie stars. Although he wasn't the first person to sing rock 'n' roll music, Elvis Presley earned the nickname "The King of Rock 'n' Roll." Buddy Holly, Chuck Berry, Eddie Cochran, and many others also became well-known names. Later, fans of British acts such as the Beatles and the Rolling Stones screamed and fainted at concerts.

As a result of its wild popularity, rock 'n' roll spawned other industries. Record companies produced or licensed special items, such as posters and pins for fans to collect. Rock 'n' rollers also inspired a culture change. Teens quickly adopted the fashions worn by their favorite artists. Many young people began plucking at electric guitars and banging on drums, hoping to follow in the footsteps of their teen idols.

Despite the popularity of rock 'n' roll with young Americans, the big recording companies at first refused to record rock acts. Only after independent record labels such as Atlantic, Sun, and Motown Records began making big profits did the larger companies follow along.

Rock music also gave the movie and TV industries a boost. Hollywood cashed in on the new craze by

Fast Fact

Record companies discovered a marketing phenomenon in the production of the "single"—a 7-inch (18-cm) disk with a big hole in the center and one song on each side. Singles, or 45s, allowed rock 'n' roll fans to buy only their favorite tunes. Songs featured on 45s often became enormous hit records, propelling the artist to stardom and increasing the profits of the recording companies.

The Phonograph

The Top of the Charts

In the 1950s, the *Billboard* pop charts began rating the popularity and success of American songs. The first rock 'n' roll record to hit the charts was "Crazy Man Crazy," by Bill Haley, in 1953. Two years later, "Rock Around the Clock," by Bill Haley and the Comets, became the first rock 'n' roll record to hit number one on the charts. The song had debuted earlier that year in the movie *Blackboard Jungle.* It remained in the number one spot for twenty-four weeks.

filming rock-related musicals starring popular singers such as Elvis Presley, Frankie Avalon, and Annette Funicello. Even films that weren't musicals often used rock music.

Rock 'n' roll hit the small screen, too. In 1957, *American Bandstand* began airing on the ABC network. The show featured stars lip-synching their hits or talking about themselves. It also showed teens in the latest fashions dancing to the hottest songs. The show was on the air until 1963 and then had a brief revival in 1989.

In 1981, the Music Television Channel (MTV) began broadcasting on cable. MTV, targeted at viewers aged twelve to thirty-four, aired nonstop music videos—mini-movies for each song. MTV transformed the recording industry. Now it wasn't enough for people to listen to a song—they wanted to see the video that went with it. An unappealing music video would not necessarily doom a song, but a good music video could make it more popular. Videos propelled singers such as Madonna and Michael Jackson into superstardom. In less than ten years, MTV boasted a viewing audience of more than forty million. MTV gradually changed its focus from music videos to game and dating shows, cartoons, and even science fiction (*Eonflux*), in order to target its viewing audience: people in their teens and twenties.

In the late 1990s, rap music became as popular with teens as rock had been in past decades. For some adolescents, rap played the same role that rock had once played in the lives of their parents: a safe means of expressing feelings of frustration and anger. Many parents were horrified to find themselves shaking their heads in disapproval at this new music genre—just as their own parents once had disapproved of rock 'n' roll decades ago.

Making Music

Today, it can take months and lots of money to record a CD. The basic formula for producing a CD is to record the songs, package them (design the cover and other material to go with them), and sell the CD. But much more goes on inside a recording studio than most people know. Making popular recordings is a combination of both science and art. Today, it is an important industry that involves many different people working together to produce the best sound possible.

The recording engineer is responsible for all the technical aspects of making a record. He or she chooses what types of recording equipment will be used and where the musicians will be seated. The recording engineer supervises the other technicians. The recording engineer and other technicians are separated from the musicians by a large glass window. As the musicians play their song, the technicians use electronic equalizing equipment to make the music sound as good as possible.

Each musician sings or plays his or her part of the song into a separate microphone, recording that part

Fast Fact

In the 1930s, the largest recording studio in the world was Abbey Road in London. Abbey Road consisted of three different studios: a large auditorium for orchestras, a medium-sized room for smaller bands, and a small room for singers and small groups. The largest recording studio today is located at the School of Audio Engineering in Byron Bay, Australia.

The Phonograph

◄ Recording engineers working on a record in a studio. Recording engineers adjust sound, tone, loudness, and quality in order to get the right "mix" of music on a record.

onto its own track. The tracks can be recorded on magnetic or digital tape or onto a computer. In some cases, certain instruments are recorded first, with other instruments and vocals added later.

In the past, musicians had to perform a song in its entirety over and over, until engineers had captured the best possible version of a song. Today, the song is usually recorded piece by piece. Then, the pieces and tracks are edited, by a process called **mixing,** into one master recording.

During this part of the recording process, engineers choose the best parts of the song to use for the final product. They can also adjust the tone and loudness of certain tracks and fix mistakes.

6 THE STATE OF SOUND TODAY

▼ *The portable compact disk player gives anyone the chance to listen to high-quality sound on the go.*

In the early 1970s, Japanese engineers developed a new way to record sound digitally. With **digital recording**, sound waves are translated from electrical signals into pieces of digital information called **samples**. Each sample is one second of sound. Each second is then given a unique binary code. A binary code is part of a mathematical language consisting of a series of zeros and ones.

In 1972, Japan's Nippon Columbia Company began making master recordings using this new digital technology. (A **master recording** is the original recording that is used to make all other copies of a tape or record.) Advances in digital recording technology continued throughout the following decades. In 1983, for example, Americans Ray Kurzweil (b. 1948) and Robert Moog (b. 1934) began selling digital **synthesizers**. These machines electronically create sounds that accurately mimic original sounds.

In 1990, Sony began selling digital audiotape (DAT) in the United States. Although digital audiotapes produce a higher-quality sound than standard magnetic tapes, DAT is incompatible with cassette technology. Consumers who prefer to use DAT must purchase all new equipment. As a result, DAT is not widely used by the average consumer.

CDs Change Everything

The year 1982 marked a major milestone in the recording industry. In Japan, compact disks, or CDs, went on sale. At 4.75 inches (12 cm), compact disks are smaller and more compact than records, yet they can hold much more information than either records or tapes.

If spread out, the continuous track on a CD stretches roughly 3 miles (4.8 kilometers). Made from metal-coated plastic, CDs also proved more durable than records or tapes. And while records and tapes both suffer damage each time they are played, CDs remain unchanged. Music recorded digitally on CDs sounds the same during the first or the thousandth playing.

▲ Electronic instruments, such as the first synthesizer Robert Moog introduced in the 1960s, can duplicate the sounds of various traditional instruments. The first commercial digital synthesizer was released by Moog in 1983.

How a CD Player Works

A CD has one long track of data that begins at the disk's center and winds its way to the outer edge. This track of digital information is located on the disk's bottom. When the disk is inserted into a CD player, it begins to spin, much faster than a record spins on a record player: CD players usually spin at either 200 rpm or 500 rpm. A laser beam at the bottom of the player scans the readable side of the disk. The beam starts at the disk's center and follows the spiral track of digital information toward the outer edge—the opposite of a record player.

The disk's metal coating reflects the light of the laser. As the laser passes over bits of digital information burned into the disk, the intensity, or strength, of the reflected light changes. A digital-to-analog converter in the CD player converts the reflected light into electrical signals. These electrical signals are then converted into sound.

CDs were created through a joint venture between the Philips Company and the Sony Corporation as a means of recording and replaying digital sound. Like wax cylinders, vinyl records, and cassette tapes, CDs require their own unique technology. Nothing makes physical contact with CDs when they are played. CDs have no grooves for reading by a stylus; instead, CD players use a laser beam to read the binary code off the disk's lower surface. A laser is a device that creates a narrow, intense beam of light. CD players also allow listeners to play songs in any order. Remote-control devices allow music lovers to change a tune from any spot in the room.

In 1983, CDs were introduced to American consumers. High prices for CD players and the CDs themselves kept initial sales volumes low. Music lovers, however, marveled at the excellent sound quality of CDs. By 1986, CDs were outselling vinyl records, and by the early 1990s, most recording studios used digital recording equipment to produce CDs.

The new disks set off a furious debate among music lovers. Many eagerly embraced the new recording format and its superior sound quality. Others, however, remained loyal to their vinyl records, claiming that their vinyl recordings sounded richer and warmer. Eventually, the argument was settled by the recording industry: Today, new vinyl records are hardly ever produced the United States.

Although CDs offered consumers a better quality of sound recording, they were at first play-only: People could not record on them.

In 1991, blank CD-Rs (recordable disks) and **CD burners** (recorders) were put on the market. This new technology allows consumers to record their own permanent CDs. CD-Rs contain a layer of dye. The CD burner's laser beam stores the digital

Fast Fact

Robert Moog, an American engineer, invented the first synthesizer in 1964. The Moog Synthesizer, as the device was known, was played like a keyboard. It made many different sounds. For example, the Moog Synthesizer mimicked existing instruments and even created new sounds not used in music before. The device created a new style of electronic music. *Switched-On Bach,* one of the first records of electronic music, was an all-synthesizer recording of music written by classical composer Johann Sebastian Bach.

Remastering Vinyl Records

As compact disks became more popular than vinyl records, the demand for old recordings in CD format grew. Companies responded by reproducing classic vinyl records in digital format. To remaster these classics, sound engineers digitally remove the scratches and other sounds on the vinyl records from the recording. Records made as long ago as the 1930s have been restored for modern listeners using this technique.

sound information by etching, or burning, patterns of pits into the dye. In 1997, CD-RWs (rewritable disks) were released. Unlike CD-Rs, CD-RWs are erasable and reusable.

Like other types of new technology, the first CD burners were expensive. In recent years, these devices gradually dropped in price, making them affordable for most people. Many computer packages now include CD-burning software as a standard feature.

The ease of Internet access allows people to upload music and other sound files on their home computers and send them to friends and family. Soon, Web sites devoted to free uploading and downloading of music were available to anyone surfing the Internet. After first downloading special software, music lovers downloaded as much music as they liked—without paying a penny. This music could be played on the computer or recorded (burned) onto a CD.

Downloading and replaying music became even easier and more economical with the introduction of MP3, a format for storing data that compresses, or squeezes, large electronic files into smaller ones. For example, sound technicians using the MP3 format can reduce a 58-megabyte file into about a 5.7-megabyte file, making it easier to send over the

The MP3

The term "MP3" is a shortened version of the name for the sound compression format used by the Motion Picture Experts Group (MPEG). The "3" in MP3 refers to "Layer Three" of a series of mathematical formulas used to encode audio electronic files for easier transmission. MP3 condenses files by recognizing and eliminating unnecessary noises that affect sound quality.

Internet. MP3 technology was developed in Germany in 1987. Today, MP3 is the standard format for digital recording.

MP3 software on a computer allows computer users to convert MP3 files into playable music. Portable MP3 players let listeners take their favorite music almost anywhere: The MP3 player is the Walkman of the twenty-first century. One of the most popular players today is the iPod by Apple Computer, Inc. Some types of iPods can store and play as many as ten thousand songs. Thanks to such versatile sound technology as iPods and CDs, disk records and cassette tapes have become virtually obsolete.

Sharing or Stealing?

Access to downloadable music on the Internet created legal and moral issues for both consumers and the music industry. For several years, people could download "free" music from Internet Web sites such as Napster and Kazaa. Although music lovers were thrilled, recording companies were not happy. Why, they wondered, would consumers pay for CDs they could download free off the Internet?

The Recording Industry Association of America (RIAA) fought to protect the rights and pocketbooks

The Jukebox Evolves

As musical times have changed, so has the jukebox. The first coin-operated phonographs played the early wax cylinders created by Edison and by Bell and Tainter. Later, as disk recordings became popular, jukeboxes were modified to play them. In 1951, for example, just two years after 45s were introduced, jukeboxes were updated to play these new disks. Today's jukeboxes play compact disks.

of recording companies and musical artists. In 1998, about two hundred recording, computer, and other tech companies joined together to start the Secure Digital Music Initiative (SDMI). SDMI's goal was to develop technology to protect digital music. In 1999, the group created voluntary technical standards for new MP3 players. The new MP3 players would not play pirated music—music downloaded illegally from the Internet.

To combat music piracy directly, RIAA also took several steps on its own. In 1999, for example, the group sued to prevent the Rio portable MP3 player from being sold. RIAA lost this court battle, however. Next, RIAA tried to shut down Web sites that offered free music. In 2000, RIAA won a federal court order to shut down the *Napster* Web site, the most popular online site for downloading free music. Finally, RIAA went after the people who downloaded music online. The

▼ *An MP3 player allows listeners to store hours of digitally recorded music on a tiny computer chip.*

▲ Left to right: Mitch Bainwol, chairman of the Recording Industry Association of America, Jack Valenti, president of the Motion Picture Association, LL Cool J, recording artist, and Mike Negra, president of Mike Video, Inc., testify before a Senate committee on illegal music file downloading in Washington, D.C., in 2003.

organization sued more than 260 people in 2003, including college students and even twelve-year-olds. Many people settled out of court in order to avoid paying thousands of dollars. Since that time, RIAA has filed more than six thousand lawsuits against file sharers.

Many Americans were outraged by the lawsuits. Some compared downloading free music to borrowing a book from the library or renting a video from the movie store. Others, however, supported the rights of the artists to collect money they were losing by not selling the albums.

Today, some record companies allow consumers to purchase music directly over the Internet. At other Web sites, Web surfers can download music after paying a fixed price for each song. And some Web sites still offer free MP3 downloads, often promoting the songs of up-and-coming artists who want exposure and publicity.

The Phonograph

The Recording Industry Continues to Grow

Despite the threat of free downloads and a 10 percent decrease in sales in the first few years of the twenty-first century, the recording industry remains healthy. Today, hundreds of recording companies around the world create millions of recordings that cater to an unparalleled variety of musical tastes. Even so, popular music—rock, rap, jazz, and country—is the recording industry's chief source of income.

Since the late 1800s, recorded sound has come a long way, from tinfoil cylinders to MP3 files. While some inventions survived, others are now found only in museums or antique shops. As sound technology continues to advance, who knows what the future holds?

The Sony Corporation

In 1945, Japanese engineer Masaru Ibuka founded a company called the Tokyo Telecommunications Research Institute in Japan. Later renamed the Sony Corporation, the company was at the cutting edge of entertainment and communication technology. In 1975, Sony created the first videocassette recorders for home use. Four years later, the company pioneered the Walkman. In 1982, Sony began selling the first CD players.

Sony entered the world of American sound recording in 1968 when it joined with CBS Records to sell music in parts of Asia. In 1980, the company bought out CBS. In the summer of 2004, Sony joined with BMG, a German company, to create one of the largest recording companies in the world. Sony-BMG Music is now the parent company of such historic record labels as Columbia, RCA Victor, Epic, and Arista. The company, headquartered in New York City, has offices all over the globe.

TIME LINE

c. 1856	Edouard-Leon Scott de Martinville invents the phonautograph.
1877	Thomas Alva Edison builds the first working phonograph.
1886	Chichester Bell and Charles Tainter invent the graphophone.
1887	Emile Berliner invents the gramophone.
1891	Edison invents the Kinetoscope, the world's first motion picture viewer.
1894	Edison invents the Kinetophone, a kinetoscope with sound added.
1898	Valdemar Poulsen invents the magnetic tape recorder, the telegraphone.
1914	Edison introduces the Telescribe, an early answering machine.
1921	*Dream Street,* the first movie to include some sound, is released.
1923	Phonofilm is invented. Vitaphone is invented.
1927	Movietone, an improved version of Phonofilm, is released. *The Jazz Singer* with Al Jolson is released by Warner Brothers.
1928	German engineer Fritz Pfleumer invents tape for sound recording. *City Lights,* the first all-talking feature film, is released.
1931	Movie sound engineers introduce the three-way speaker system.
1935	Bell Laboratories introduces a tape answering machine.
1945	In Japan, the company that will eventually become Sony is founded.
1948	Columbia introduces the 33⅓ rpm record.
1949	The Radio Corporation of America (RCA) introduces the 45 rpm record.
1958	The eight-track tape and player are introduced.
1963	The Philips Company begins manufacturing cassette tapes.
1964	Robert Moog invents the first electronic synthesizer.
1966	Ray Dolby invents a tape player that reduces hissing sounds.
1970	Blank cassette tapes are put on the market.
1972	Nippon Columbia Company begins making digital master recordings.
1979	The Sony Walkman is born.
1982	Compact disks go on sale in Japan.
1987	MP3 technology is developed in Germany.
1991	Blank CD-R disks and CD burners are put on the market.
2000	A federal court orders *Napster* to shut down.
2003	Recording companies begin suing people who continue to download free music from the Internet.
2005	Apple Computer, Inc., introduces the iPod Shuffle Random Music Player.

GLOSSARY

amplifiers: devices that increase the strength of an electrical signal

CD burners: machines that record information onto a compact disk

cinematograph: an early film projection machine

digital recording: a sound-recording process in which sound waves are translated from electrical signals into pieces of digital information

gramophone: the first phonograph to play flat disk records, invented in 1893

graphophone: a machine, built in 1886, that improved upon Edison's phonograph

Kinetograph: an early camera used to make motion pictures

Magnetophon: an early tape recorder that used lightweight paper tape

master recording: the original recording that is used to make all other copies of a tape, record, or CD

mixing: the process of editing and improving a sound recording

Movietone: a system of sound recording in which the sound track was included on the film itself, next to the picture frames

phonautograph: an early machine used to record sound waves and produce a visual image of the sound

Phonofilm: a type of movie film with a strip of sound recording on its edge

phonograph: a machine that reproduces sound by means of a stylus in contact with a grooved rotating disk

quadraphonic sound: sound that is recorded with four different microphones and played back on four different speakers

rpm: revolutions per minute

samples: pieces of digital information used in digital sound recording

sound tracks: the strips on movie films that contain the words, music, and other sounds

splicing: editing a tape by cutting out an unwanted part and joining the new edges of the tape together

stereophonic sound: sound that is recorded with two or more micro-phones, then played back on two or more speakers

stylus: a needle used in early phonographs to record and play sound waves

synthesizers: machines that create sounds electronically

telegraphone: the first tape recorder

tracks: strips on a tape or record on which sound is recorded

Vitaphone: a sound system that involved playing a recorded musical disk on a phonograph synchronized with a movie

FOR MORE INFORMATION

Books

Ashley, Susan. *Yo-Yo Ma.* Trailblazers of the Modern World. Milwaukee, Wisconsin: World Almanac Library, 2005.

Brown, Adele Q. *Elvis Presley.* Trailblazers of the Modern World. Milwaukee, Wisconsin: World Almanac Library, 2003.

Burgan, Michael. *The Beatles.* Trailblazers of the Modern World. Milwaukee, Wisconsin: World Almanac Library, 2002.

Hantula, Richard. *Thomas Edison.* Trailblazers of the Modern World. Milwaukee, Wisconsin: World Almanac Library, 2005.

Holland, Gini. *Louis Armstrong.* Trailblazers of the Modern World. Milwaukee, Wisconsin: World Almanac Library, 2004.

Parker, Steve. *Sound.* Langhorne, Pennsylvania: Chelsea House, 2004.

Videos and DVDs

The History of Rock 'n' Roll. Burbank, CA: Warner Home Video, 2004.

Music and Technology. South Burlington, VT: Pacific Street Films and the Educational Film Center, 2000.

Pioneers of Cinema. New York: WinStar Home Entertainment, 1999.

Recording History. Princeton, NJ: Films for the Humanities & Sciences, 1998.

Thomas Edison. Irving, TX: Nest Entertainment, 2001.

Web Sites

http://memory.loc.gov/ammem/berlhtml/berlhome.html This Library of Congress Web site contains fascinating information on Emile Berliner and his role in the birth of the recording industry.

http://memory.loc.gov/ammem/edhtml/edhome.html This Library of Congress Web site is devoted to Thomas Alva Edison and his influence on the entertainment industry.

www.recording-history.org/ The Sound Recording Technology Web site offers a history of the phonograph, the cassette tape, and many other recording devices.

www.uspto.gov/web/offices/ac/ahrpa/opa/kids/special/kidbright.html The Web site of the U.S. Patent Office offers information on patents and the inventors who shaped history.

INDEX

Author Biography

Robin Doak is a writer of fiction and nonfiction books for children, ranging from elementary to high school levels. She writes about many topics, including the human body, profiles of U.S. presidents, athletes, and American immigration. Robin is a former editor of *Weekly Reader* and, in addition to her extensive experience writing for children, has also written numerous support guides for educators. Robin holds a bachelor of arts degree in English from the University of Connecticut.